From the Darkness To My Story

Never Let the World Stop You From Being You

Wilma Rodriguez

Copyright © 2023

All Rights Reserved

Dedication

To my grandchildren, children, husband, family, and friends.

To all the amazing people I have met, those I haven't, and those still battling the darkness.

"Be Happy. Be You. Be Bright."

Acknowledgment

This work would not have been possible without the support of the Publishing Company The Writing Cube. Special thank you to Stella Rose and the entire team that made this possible.

I'm grateful to all of those with whom I've had the pleasure of sharing this project.

Nobody has been more important to me in the pursuit of this project than my husband & the members of my family & friends. Big thank you to all.

Andy Rodriguez
Gloria Rodriguez
Andrew Rodriguez
Robinson Morales
Lynn Disalvatore
Jennifer Ortiz DeViliate
Raquedys Villalona

CONTENTS

Dedication iii

Acknowledgment iv

About the Author vi

What Inspired Me To Write This Book viii

Chapter 1 1

Chapter 2 5

Chapter 3 12

Chapter 4 19

Chapter 5 22

About the Author

You won't meet a woman like Wilma twice.

She is both the calm and the storm. She has been through a lot, but even through these tough times, she paints a pretty face over her tears and gives her all to her family. She has been betrayed before, so it takes a while for her heart to soften, but once she lets you in, she is ride-or-die loyal.

Wilma has learned a lot over the last few years, and she's wasted too much time allowing others to backseat the drive in her life—now she's in control. She continues to rise—again and again.

Born: Brooklyn, New York, US. January 20, 1973

Age: 50

Occupation: Medical and Judicial interpreter

Spouse: Andy Rodriguez

Children: Victor Santos, Sergio Santos, Diaselmi K. Santos, Maria Rodriguez

Grandchildren: Annalisa Santos, Christian Santos, Adrian Santos, Jacob Salazar, Camila Flakes, Jordyn Flakes, Nova Vargas.

Relatives: (As noted in the book.)

In-laws + Rodriguez Family

What Inspired Me To Write This Book

A desire to change people the way they see the world. To make them feel understood, to deliver hope, to motivate them, to be positive, to make them feel valuable, and to teach them to never give up in life no matter their situation—to teach them that nothing in life is impossible.

I wrote this book to finally close a chapter in my life that was open for many years, leaving emptiness and sadness inside, so I decided to write this book to become stronger. Life is called life for a reason: life is sharing and caring, which means leaving behind lessons learned in hopes that others will learn from it, which was my goal in writing this book.

Page Blank Intentionally

Chapter 1

I was born in Brooklyn, NY, in 1973. At the age of two, I migrated with my parents to Puerto Rico, where I grew up with my six other siblings, four sisters and two brothers. However, I always felt rejected by my family members. My sisters never shared their toys, clothes, etc., with me. They always called me names and blamed me for all the bad things that happened at our house. I never interacted with my brothers as much. All my siblings were there for each other, but I always felt I was the "ugly duckling." In short, I had no close relationship with any of my siblings.

Even my father never gave me love; I always felt I wasn't his daughter because of how he spoke or treated me. My mother never did anything about it because she always wanted to be good in front of her husband, so she also preferred to reject me.

I never asked for anything. I only wanted one thing: to be loved. But I was bullied both in school and at home. However, I never let that bother me and continued doing what I was supposed to. Going to school every day and getting good grades was "my father's" pride and the only thing he wanted from me. He never showed me any sign of love, hugged, or even kissed me.

My father never liked his father-in-law, so I always thought this was the only reason he never liked me because I used to resemble my grandfather.

Moreover, my elder sister used to bully and insult me. She only preferred to be nicer to her friends than to her own sister. The clothes that she didn't want to wear anymore, she used to sell them to me, and if I didn't have enough money to buy them, she would chop them up and throw them away. She was very mean to me, and her cold behavior made me sad. However, I always kept things to myself and never fought or said anything. I preferred to stay quiet, hoping my family would accept and love me someday.

I used to come from school to study. However, I couldn't because even though there were seven of us, I was the only one to do all the work at home (cleaning, taking the garbage out, etc.). None of my siblings ever offered to help. I had to do it all on my own. If I ever told my father that I needed to study so that he could send someone else, he would force me to do the chores. Therefore, I had no other choice but to do it, no matter what. No one cared, even if I had to prepare for the test that would take place the next day. I had to complete the chores first.

My father even treated my mother poorly. He was always unfaithful to her, but my mother was always there. He was also a little abusive with me and sometimes, with one of my brothers, would make me get on my knees on a metal lid with holes made with nails. He would also make me pee on hot rocks and walk on hot coals.

On top of that, whenever I used to get sick, they never took me to the doctor. They used to cure me at home. One day, I got an ear infection. I was suffering from sharp and sudden pain and had trouble falling asleep. As expected, my father didn't take me to the doctor. However, he did something that was beyond anyone's expectations. He made one of my cousins pee in my ears. It was disgusting! However, one thing was certain: I never got an ear infection after that.

This is nothing compared to what I will tell you next. When I was eight years old, my father once told me I would be a gun with no papers, meaning I would be a prostitute. I was shocked at what he had told me. How could someone who brought me into this world say something so mean to me? What was my fault? Why was I being treated like that? This shattered me, and I broke into tears.

Chapter 2

That day I think I transformed from an innocent little girl to the one that was about to become stronger. Those words were the ones that gave me the strength and power not to give up. It was terrible because my mother was beside him, but she did nothing or say anything.

I used to go to school every day and made many "good friends," who are still my friends until this day. I used to feel so lucky just because I had some good company, at least there. I used to go to their house with them after school because I hated going back home, but as soon as I would go home, my father used to wait for me at the door with his belt to beat me up and punish me.

When I was 10 years old, I had a job. I used to clean one of my teacher's windows to have money for my stuff. She hired me for $2 per week. My siblings did what they wanted and had no restrictions. I never understood why my parents never said anything to them. I always asked myself if we were all family, why wouldn't they treat me like my other siblings?

My siblings used to get new clothes for every school year, and I got their old ones. Once when my sister turned 15, she got a great party with all her friends at my grandma's. My grandmother loved her just as she loved my mother—my father's family only loved my big sister. So they all left before me on the party day, and I was home alone.

They were all dressed up nicely, and I did not have anything to wear, so I put on an old skirt from school and borrowed my sister's shirt without telling her. I could already imagine how mad she would be at me! But I had no choice because I was going to a party and had to wear some good clothes. I was ready to face the consequences.

And just as I had expected, she got mad at me when I got to the party because this used to happen every time I wore something from her wardrobe. She pinched me in front of people and told me to take it off. I was in tears and so ashamed that I wished for the ground to swallow me right then and there. Then I had to sit outside in a tent while everyone else inside was enjoying. I was embarrassed by how I looked at that party. I wasn't dressed properly. One of my aunts asked to take pictures with me. I was so happy that, finally, someone wanted to spend some time and make memories with me. However, my sister arrived at that very moment, and she restricted my aunt to not to take any pictures with me, but she should only take pictures with her friends.

Now when I had turned 15, there was no party at our house. I asked to be taken to church just to get blessed. And I still remember being in summer school and never having summers off. Even when I was in kindergarten, got sick, didn't want to go, or cried, my mother beat me up and ripped my clothes off. So I had to go to school all year round.

But as the days passed, I became sick and tired of the bad treatment, name-calling, no love, and bullying. So, I decided to escape the house in 1986. I got so frustrated that I made a plan with one of my best friends from high school. That morning felt like none other. I was excited yet scared. Before leaving for school, I remember telling my mother I'll see you next year. However, she told me not to say that and simply said bye. So, I left for school.

So, I left for the USA by myself with a school bag full of books and came to New Jersey. I was just 15 years old in a town of complete strangers. And this new city life made me feel like I was always a part of their family. However, when my family realized I was missing, they looked for me in my friends' houses, schools, etc., but no one knew where I was. Then they heard from one of my friends that I had left. They couldn't believe what I had done to them. But I had to go because they always thought about themselves, never about me.

So they all called and insulted me. But guess what? There was nothing that they could have said. So I knew I was getting stronger day by day. Then I started school, finished high school, and met a guy. We moved in together and had three beautiful children, two boys, and a girl. We both loved each other and the little family that we had created.

My parents never cared for him when I had my first child. Later, when my son was 6 months old, I went back to them to introduce him to them. Still, they did not acknowledge my child or me, so I returned to Jersey and stayed with my boyfriend. Then I had another baby boy, and this second child had kidney issues. When he was born, I needed to get him operated on urgently. The doctors told me that we needed blood, so of course, I called my family. I asked them to come there and help me with the baby as I couldn't donate blood because I was underweight and my son needed surgery. But no one came to donate blood for my seven-month baby. Something I will never forget! But thank God he did not need it in the end.

Then I had a baby girl. After a couple of years, I started having problems with my children's father because he cheated on me. We broke up, and he left me on the street with my three children and all the debts.

Then I lived in a motel room for two weeks till I got a small apartment and started working three jobs to raise my children as a single mother. By then, my family had already moved here, and they all had apartments, but none took me in. They did not care about my problems or what I was going through. I kept working and doing the best for my children and me. I met a lot of people over the years while I was learning about life. But I always loved my family no matter what had happened in the past. I never held grudges or hate for anyone. I always loved my mother, even though she never gave me the love I always craved from her.

So, I worked three jobs. Then I finally got a small apartment for my children and me. I struggled a lot, but I always encouraged myself to keep going and never give up. For my children, I was a mother before a woman. I had my firstborn at the age of 18, the second at 19, and my daughter at 23. I did not want my children to feel neglected like I always did during my childhood.

The English language was a big barrier for me in the beginning. Many people also bullied my Spanish accent, but I never let that break down my walls. I always kept my head up high and looked forward. I had never let anyone put me down, even if they

From the Darkness to My Story - Never Let the World Stop You From Being You

tried.

Chapter 3

One day I met the love of my life, but he also put me through a lot of pain because he was going through a lot himself. So, I told myself I could help him. In fact, we both could help each other. He was going through his divorce, got custody of his daughter, and I had my three children. We both fell in love, made everything work out, and got married. With him, I finally gave our children a stable home, and one of my dreams finally came true: a family and a home full of love.

However, I was still dealing with family issues even after being married. I had a life that still made me suffer because I always thought about why my family never loved me, so I went for counseling. After examining everything, the counselor concluded that I was a (bastard) child because of how they treated me over the years. But I still looked for them and was always there. I didn't want to regret anything. They always criticized me, talked badly about me to other people, and never called my kids. There was envy, jealousy, etc.

I never understood why (there is the question again) my older sister mistreated my mother. She was mean to her. She snapped her fingers, and my mother had to run to do things for her till the day she passed. It was crazy.

I remember when I was getting married to my fiancée. I called them because, of course, I wanted my family at my wedding. They told me they couldn't come because they had nothing to wear, so I had to dress them all so they could be at my wedding with me.

They never informed me of the passing of any family member, as if it was not my problem. On the same day of my wedding, I took my mother in the morning with me to get our nails done. So, I asked her about my grandma, and she told me that my grandmother had passed on the same day a year ago. Crazy to say; I was shocked!

Also, they only looked for me when they wanted something, a party, money, a favor, etc. I was only good enough for that.

On holidays there was never a gift for my children or myself, not that I expected, but my mother had other grandkids she always loved and cared for, except mine. Be it Mother's Day or Christmas, I cried every holiday. I sobbed because I just wanted my family and the love that I had always craved from them.

One day my mother got sick. Something was bothering her. She had pain in the side of her leg, because of which she could not walk. So, they came to my house and asked if I could take her to the doctor because none of my siblings spoke English. Only I was the one who had learned it over the years. Another thing I did not mention was that when my mother moved here, she lived with my younger sister.

So, as I was saying previously, they knocked at my door. It was my brother, sister, and mother. They had some paper from the doctors and then told me our mother had this pain that was not going away. He asked me to take her to the doctor and read the test results from the previous day. So that made my mother stay with me. But as I grabbed the results and read them myself, I learned that my mother did not have pain in her side as they thought for a long time, but they took her for granted for a serious condition that was taking over her body.

My mother had Bone Cancer, Stage 4. I was heartbroken when I found out my mother had been living with my sister, taking care of my niece, while my sister was treating her like shit. But my mother was always there no matter what. I found the best oncologist for my mother and took her to the doctor. They put her on treatment. When the doctor asked for all my mother's results, I asked my sister for them, and she handed me a bunch of hospital letters about missing appointments. I learned that she never followed up with my mother's doctors. If only she had cared for our mother, she would not have had cancer because it went from her breast to her bones.

So, after all the good treatment with the new oncologist, my sister forced me to change doctors for my mother, and neglected her, missing her appointments and medicines. My mother slowly started to get sick again. They called me to go with her to the hospital while I was working a full-time job. Regardless, I took her to the hospital, where she was admitted for her treatment again. I drove every day to see my mother and help her with the doctors.

One day my mother called me out of the blue.

"Please, can you come and help me? Your sister doesn't understand the doctors, and if they said they needed to cut my leg, she would say yes," my mother said to me.

My mother was scared because of a huge language barrier and had already gotten many surgeries she didn't need.

The day she called me, I was very sick in bed with the flu. I did not want to drive because I had a fever. I was tired, so I called my son and asked him to take me to the hospital because I couldn't drive at that moment.

From the Darkness to My Story - Never Let the World Stop You From Being You

My son came, took me, and drove me to the hospital. It was raining cats and dogs, so going out was a bad idea. However, I still managed to go and visit my mother. When we got to the hospital, my mother was sitting on her bed. She looked at me desperately and begged me that she didn't want another surgery. I assured her it would be alright and asked her where the doctor was.

However, when I spoke to him, he explained to me that she needed this surgery. Therefore, I explained to my mother that she would be just fine.

"I told your sister not to leave me alone, but she left," she told me.

"Don't worry. Everything will be ok. I will be here tomorrow," I comforted her.

My mother went into surgery the next day but never woke up again. I was heartbroken and very devastated. Finally, when I began to have a healthy relationship with my mother, she left me. My son and I were the last ones who saw her alive. The doctors left a needle in my mother's artery for nine hours, and my mother had a stroke. This was medical malpractice. My mother was in ICU for two weeks, just on life support, hooked to a machine even though she had no movement. She was in a vegetable state—she was never going to recover.

The doctors and the neurologists were doing all kinds of tests to see if there were any changes, but there was nothing. Therefore, they came to the conclusion that it was time to disconnect my mother and send her to hospice.

Chapter 4

When all that was happening, we were all in the hospital, waiting, going through the same pain, but my brothers and sisters thought that only they were the ones suffering from this, not me. So they left my mother hooked to the tube for two weeks before the doctors spoke to everyone that they needed someone to make a decision and put my mother in hospice.

No one else wanted to sign the papers, so of course, it was all up to me. They all signed an agreement for me to sign for my mother to be taken off the machine. I signed, and then my mother was taken to hospice. I was there with her for 16 hours, with no food or sleep. I came home the following morning and, only 15 minutes later, received a call to tell me that she was gone. She passed away on 31 January 2017.

After all that happened, all my brothers and sisters blamed me that I was the one who had killed our mother. My sister even told my eight-year-old niece that I had killed her grandmother.

When we got together for the funeral arrangements, we took her to P.R., where she was born. We did the services there—it was very painful and sad.

After all that had happened, my brother divorced his wife of seven years because of them and left and denied his own daughter in court. He left his wife on the street with my niece and her son, and my family did nothing to stop his mean behavior but instead participated and aided him with the divorce, even though that was our niece. I was there for my sister-in-law and helping her, and they hated me for it. It has been seven years that she has been gone, and I did not—nor do I want to—hear anything from them.

I never needed them, and I don't hate them—I do not hold grudges against them. I wish them the best, but I want them to be far away from me.

The last thing they did was that they all got together—they were always together—and went to P.R., moved my mother from her grave, and buried her somewhere else. To this day, they haven't told me where she is. You do not do that to your worst enemy. As a result, I cannot visit my mother because I don't know where her grave is.

Because I was never really loved by my parents or siblings, I did not believe that love really existed for the longest time. So whenever someone used to tell me that they loved me, I would not believe them. For a long time, I was afraid of rejection and had severe trust issues. I created a wall around my heart that sealed those feelings inside me so that while they were still present, they were not obvious to the other person.

Rejection for me is very painful.

When I met my husband and got together with him, there was a time when I felt he did not love me like he said he did, and I assumed he was with me because he pitied me. It took me a while to realize it was not true, but I eventually got there.

You can, too, come out of darkness.

Chapter 5

Over the years, I have grown as a person; I have a good job, I have many certifications, and plenty of great friends, some of whom I consider to be my family.

I'm a happily married woman with three adult children, one stepdaughter, and seven grandchildren that are my life.

I have people who envy me, are jealous of me, and are always trying to put me down, but I don't let these things affect me now.

I keep moving forward, fighting for what I want.

I want to thank all my elementary school friends—the ones who I am no longer in touch with and the ones I am still in touch with—who were there since the beginning of it all, the real friends and the fake ones, too, because you all have been a part of my journey.

I always wondered if the man I call my "father," the

man who raised me, was not my real father because of how he treated me. I asked him a couple of times, but the conversation got changed or ignored. He was always only looking for money or anything else that he needed. I wasn't sure why, but I never trusted him or the way he looked at me when I was younger. I never understood why, but my heart always told me they were hiding something from me.

It was probably one of those cases when, back in the day, if a woman got pregnant, she would be sent away to have the child. Given how I was treated, I thought that's what happened to my mother. We were seven brothers and sisters; six of them were born in P.R., and one in Brooklyn, NY – I was the odd one out—the ugly duckling.

I have nieces and nephews who have no idea who I am because my brothers and sisters chose not to tell their children about me. On one occasion, my sister-in-law stole from me, and they all still sided with her instead of me, even when there was concrete proof. I lost the only brother I was close to because of this.

I now have beautiful people in my life. I have been through a lot but never abandoned my faith in God. I always say, "With God, everything; without God, nothing."

I have studied hard for myself and my children to give them the life they deserve and the life I never had, full of respect, love, and security. A life where we're always there for each other no matter what. I am extremely proud of the person I am now: the mother, the wife, and the friend.

One day, I just decided to stop being good to them and start being good to myself, and I haven't looked back since. I want to thank my husband, my children, and my friends for being by my side through the ups and the downs and my readers for listening to my stories and staying with me.

I just want to inspire other people and help them understand that we can move forward and make our dreams come true, no matter what happened in their past. We are unique.

Going through what I've been through is what has made me a pillar of strength for many people. I'm often under a lot of stress, but you'll never catch me without a smile on my face, no matter how exhausted I am. I have experienced a lot of pain, all of which made me stronger and more cautious. Whoever is loved by me is the luckiest person, and I am fortunate to be loved by all the people I am loved by. But it's not what's made me who I am now—it was my hard work all along. Because, like the sun, I alone can still shine.

To Be Continued...

Wilma Rodriguez

Wilma As A Kid:

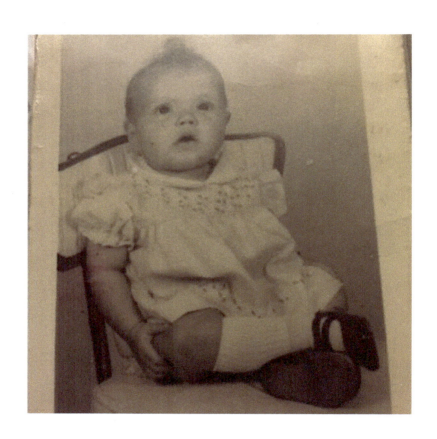

From the Darkness to My Story - Never Let the World Stop You From Being You

Wilma's Wedding Picture:

Wilma Rodriguez

Wilma's Kids When They Were Young:

From the Darkness to My Story - Never Let the World Stop You From Being You

Wilma with Andy:

Wilma Rodriguez

Wilma with Andy:

From the Darkness to My Story - Never Let the World Stop You From Being You

Wilma with Andy:

Wilma Rodriguez

Wilma with Andy:

From the Darkness to My Story - Never Let the World Stop You From Being You

Wilma with Andy:

Wilma Rodriguez

Wilma With Her Kids:

From the Darkness to My Story - Never Let the World Stop You From Being You

Wilma's Grandchildren:

Wilma Rodriguez

Wilma's Kids: